How to Attract Clients
John Gordon Duncan
Copyright © 2020 by (Capitalize Books)

All rights reserved. No part of this book may be reproduced or transmitted in any form or by any means without written permission from the author.

www.jgordonduncan.com
www.capitalize.biz

Dedication

This effort is dedicated to my wonderful wife, Amy Duncan. She believes in me and supports my dreams. I could not ask for more.

Thanks, Ames. I love you!
Gordon

Contents

Introduction 5
Networking Groups 10
Networking Events 18
Cold Calls 22
Social Media Posts 25
Educational Emails 29
Prospecting Emails 33
Final Thoughts 36

Introduction

As I made my transition from a full-time minister/part-time business owner to full-time business owner/part-time minister, I enlisted the help of a group of friends. In fact, this group became essential to my sanity during the Covid-19 quarantine. They gave me wise counsel, and they were the select few who knew my plan for a career change.

My wife and I, along with these two other couples, would meet each Saturday night on Zoom for an hour or so. We are all roughly in the same place of life and roughly the same age.

And…none of these folks own a business. They are ministry families, but I felt like I needed their input most importantly as I made the transition from the pulpit to the market place.

When I finally made my decision and made the announcement, we got together on Zoom. They asked about my company's future, and I shared with everyone how we had put in several huge proposals in the past few days and that the future looked bright.

One of the families who has a son starting a videography business asked me, "Gordon, how do people find you?"

At first, I thought she was asking about our company's website or social media pages. But no, she wanted to know how these and other potential clients found us. She wanted to know how they came to us to do business.

She cared about our future, and she wanted to know for her son's sake as well.

I explained that these proposals came from connections we had made through networking groups and my wife's book club. I also explained that our company was heavily involved in the local Chamber of Commerce and that many of our proposals and contracts came through them.

But of course, there is a lot more than that. People find us through our emails, social media posts, videos, seminars, networking groups, events, and lots more.

Then I thought, "Lots of people might want to know the answer to that question."

So, I decided to share these tactics with you in this small book so that it might be helpful for you and your business. If followed, these tried and true techniques will help you grow your business and help you achieve your dreams.

So, don't give up today when you are discouraged. Keep reaching out, putting out great content, and eventually, your clients will find you.

Gordon Duncan, Co-Owner
Capitalize/CTP Marketing
and Consulting
gordon@ctpmarketplace.com
www.capitalize.biz

Networking Groups

Networking groups are foundational for any business. They provide an instant community of like-minded professionals who want to grow their businesses and their skills. They also, when done right, provide an avenue to find new customers.

But be warned: If you only join a networking group to gain more customers, then everyone else will hold you at a distance because they will see you as a parasite or perceive you as a non-contributor.

Instead, you have to join and be a contributor.

So, how do you become a contributor and not a parasite?

Simple: Contribute.

Ask others how you can support them.

Learn about the other business professionals personally.

Don't immediately offer your services.

Focus on personal growth and not business growth.

But you might ask, "Then, why join any of these groups if all I'm doing is contributing?"

Simple. As you do this, and if you do it genuinely, then people will trust you. They will see you as someone who cares and serves. And someone who cares and serves is someone that people want to do business with.

Let me give you an example of this type of networking group. There are so many different types, but for this moment, let's talk about the local Chamber of Commerce.

I know some people think that groups like the Chamber of Commerce are old and outdated, but I disagree.

Why?

Well, according to the Center for Responsive Politics, the Chamber is the largest lobbying group in the U.S., spending more money than any other lobbying organization on a yearly basis. Chambers affect government policy nationally and locally. These folks are the movers and shakers of our country. So, enough of that.

Join a Chamber of Commerce.

Once you join, the right question to ask is, "How do I network within a Chamber?" Most all chambers have these opportunities (and so do most other networking groups).

You can…

Attend Events Celebrating Other Businesses – These are events like ribbon cuttings, grand openings, or holiday celebrations. When these businesses see you there, they will know you care.

Become a Member of a LeadShare – A LeadShare is a group that is industry-specific (one person per industry) that is committed to each other's growth and to sharing leads. Do this, and recommend people to the other people's businesses.

Some even have companies give presentations, and those presentations are great opportunities to gain new clients and improve your speaking abilities.

Serve – All of these groups have service needs. There are lots of opportunities to serve like:

Give blood at one of their blood drives

Serve at one of their large events

Lead a LeadShare

And on and on. If you serve, the Chamber will remember you. And when they remember you, they recommend you.

Attend Their Large Events – Every Chamber has socials and special events. Mine specifically has one large event at the end of each month. It is hosted by a member business, has great food/drinks, and is 95% social. Why not attend, meet new members, and connect with local businesses? Consistently attended, these events are a win for helping people find you and your business.

On a quick note, it is important to figure out which type of networking groups to avoid. The answer is simple. If they are too expensive and are too pushy, avoid them.

If they are that way with you before you join, imagine how bad they will be once you become a member.

Go for free or go for the ones whose membership fees are practical.

Networking Events

Networking events are coordinated gatherings with the intention of connecting businesses and business professionals.

Done well, these events allow you to meet new people while also letting them get to know who you are and what you do. Done poorly, they are a waste of time and money.

How do you know which is which?

First, find out who is coordinating the event.

Ask around and find out how the experience has been for those who have attended before.

Ask if the event is a bait and switch – inviting you in, offering no value, and pitching you for services or money. Avoid those.

Ask if anyone has ever gained new business from the event.

Secondly, if you choose to go, be prepared.

Bring business cards and handouts.

Make sure your website and social media pages are good to go.

Be prepared to answer any questions.

Think through what you want people to know about you, and think through what people might ask when they first hear about you.

Third, attend ready to learn about everyone else. The attendee who only advertises themselves will either be quickly forgotten or remembered only for being selfish.

An example of an event like this is happening as I write these words. In the local coffee shop that I frequent, a business housewives (their title) event is happening.

These are local business owners who work from home while also taking care of their children. They meet quarterly to share stories, encourage each other, and to talk about growing their businesses.

The event is free, the coffee is good, and the encouragement is high. It's a great event to network.

So, if you do your homework, attend regularly, get to know other professionals, you can gain new clients for your company.

Cold Calls

This is the hidden gold mine of prospecting that almost nobody will do. Everyone who doesn't do it hates it and finds lots of excuses for skipping it. Excuses like:

Cold Calling is an out of date form of prospecting.

No one wants a cold call.

I'm no good at it.

Or what I hear most often…

I refuse to cold call!

But think about cold calling this way.

When you join an organization like a Chamber of Commerce or a civic organization like Rotary, they create a directory. That directory goes out to everyone.

That means that everyone in that directory has given you permission to talk to them.

So, call them.

Think of it this way.

Let's say you call 100 people. It takes you 4 hours to call 100 people. 10 of them are willing to talk to you. 1 of them does business with you.

Then, do the math, and it makes sense. Every time you spend 4 hours calling people, you get a new client. If I told you that if you worked 4 hours to get a client, I bet you would be willing to do it. So, do it.

The only real challenge at that point is continually finding phone numbers to call.

That goes back to the point of joining a networking group like the chamber or a civic group like the Rotary. These organizations are private, and membership gives you access to people to call.

Cold calling is really about discipline. Once you get someone on the line, be genuine, tell them who you are, and ask for a meeting.

Social Media Posts

Please hear me when I say this. It is what I tell all of our social media clients (and anyone who will listen).

Everyone can do social media.

But not everyone can do social media.

So, yes, you can use social media to attract clients, but it is a long slow process. Don't fall into the trap of thinking that you can just set up a page, start posting, and attract clients. It is going to take a lot more than that.

Social media will attract clients, but there are a few of the steps you have to take if you want your social media efforts to be effective.

First, make sure your profiles are attractive. Make sure the photos fit the recommended sizes. Just Google, "Facebook profile photo size" and you'll find it. Same for cover photos. Then do that for your Instagram profiles, and all other subsequent platforms.

Use quality photos that communicate who you and your business are. Make sure all of your contact information is correct and up to date.

Second, don't hammer your followers with, "Buy from

me…do business with me," posts constantly.
Who wants anything to do with that? You don't. Why would you think anyone else would?

What that means is that social media works best to attract clients when there is something attractive about you and your business.

Constant, "Do business with us," ain't it.

So, create a strategy. That strategy should include:

Helping potential clients with their problems.

Educating them about potential pitfalls they might face.

Creating a sense of openness and interaction with you and your brand.

And when you do ask for their business, do it gently with the hope to help them affordably and kindly.

Finally, be patient on social media. For most folks, going viral doesn't happen. That means that impact and reach are long, slow processes.

You are going to have to be consistent over a long period of time and provide immense value for someone to want to do business with you merely because of social media.

Educational Emails

Educational emails are another lost art of prospecting. They are a lot like cold calls. They are effective if done well. But let's be honest. This is one of the most difficult techniques for prospecting clients. That makes sense. Results don't come easy

An educational email is when you write a regular series of emails that do exactly what they say they do: educate.

You see an educational email is one that gives value to the reader. The reader walks away knowing more than they did before reading.

The first challenge is to get anyone to even open it. Then, you have to convince them to read it. How do you do that? The answer is to approach this email like you would writing your child's teacher. Here is the format:

Your subject line should be 2-5 words like, "Make More Money at Work." At most, say, "We can help you make more money at work."

Begin with a greeting that's simple like, "Good Morning."

The body of your email should be short and to the point and less than 400 words.

Include a proper closing like, "Thank you," or, "Sincerely."
And then, include your name, phone number, and perhaps a web address.

Of course, it goes without saying to run that whole email through Grammarly or have someone check it for typos and misspellings.

But none of this will matter if the body of your email doesn't educate. This is going to take planning or maybe even an outside company. But the rules here are the same as social media. All of your emails can't be, "Buy from me," or, "Do business with me."

Educate them, and if you have a small pitch, include it in the bottom of the email or after your sign-off. Now, do this at least weekly for weeks, months, and years.

So many people quit after an email or two, but the point here is to present yourself as an expert in the field that they can trust. This doesn't happen overnight. It is a long, slow process, but it will work, and it will bring you in new clients.

Just don't give up!

Prospecting Emails

Okay, I'll be honest with you, prospecting emails are the least effective form of attracting clients, but they do work.

The priority here is to not spend too much time on them, so you can invest your time in more effective techniques, but my advice is don't abandon this effort.

Here is one example of a prospecting email.

Hello,

My name is <u>your name</u>. We are <u>who your company is and what you do.</u>

We realize the quickly changing landscape for our local businesses has presented some challenges. We want our local businesses to be successful and grow despite these challenges, so we <u>detail what your company can do for them.</u>

I would be grateful if we could meet for lunch or coffee, so I could learn more about your business and explore the possibility of a partnership.

Please let me know when we can connect. Thank you, and I look forward to <u>talking to you.</u>

Your Name
Your Phone Number
Website

Now, these do work, but you have to be patient, and you have to send out a lot of these emails.

A lot of them.

But here is the biggest point I have for you about prospect emails.

Don't burn a hot lead with a prospect email. If you have a prior relationship with a potential client, don't make a prospect email your first contact. They may dismiss you or make up their mind about you ahead of time. Save prospect emails for clients that you don't have a relationship with already.

Final Thoughts

I finished writing this on the cusp of leaving one career, growing a business, revitalizing a failing one, and launching a brand-new company.

Writing this was helpful for me because it reminded me of all that I need to do every day. No matter how busy and successful my company (or yours) ever gets, you have got to keep prospecting.

Why? Because if the pipeline is dry, your business will die.

On a day to day basis, I'm more excited about the number of potential clients we reach out to in a day than I am about the number of proposals we send out.

Why?

Because, as long as we reach out to potential clients, I know that the business will keep growing.

So, hang in there. There is no magic formula. Pick one of these approaches or all of them.

Just be consistent.

Let me know if I can help.

Gordon Duncan, Co-Owner
Capitalize/CTP Marketing
and Consulting
gordon@ctpmarketplace.com
www.capitalize.biz

Made in the USA
Middletown, DE
26 July 2024

58030101R00024